dabble lab

PUT ON A SHOW
→ WITH ←

CARDBOARD
(& DUCT TAPE)

BY

LESLIE MANLAPIG

4D™

AN AUGMENTED READING
CARDBOARD
EXPERIENCE

CAPSTONE PRESS
a capstone imprint

TABLE OF CONTENTS

Download the Capstone 4D app!

STEP 1 Ask an adult to search in the Apple App Store or Google Play for "Capstone 4D".

STEP 2 Click Install (Android) or Get, then Install (Apple).

STEP 3 Open the app.

STEP 4 Scan any of the following spreads with this icon:

Watch some fun videos!

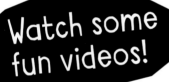

When you scan a spread, you'll find fun extra stuff to go with this book! You can also find these things on the web at www.capstone4D.com using the password: cardboard.show

YOUR ADVENTURE STARTS ↓ HERE ↓↓

Have you ever dreamed of putting on a show in front of an audience? This book will help you do all that and more, using . . .

CARDBOARD!

⇒ Yes, that's right! ⇐

The boxes sitting around your house can be used to make your very own adventures. All you need are some simple supplies and a willing adult to → help you with sharp tools.

Don't forget to check out the 4D videos to help guide you through the steps. Also, we've included many templates to help you complete projects in this book. Just scan this star! →
Before you know it, you'll be playing music and accepting an Academy Award!

-CLAP-   -CLAP-
-CLAP-

SUPPLIES

hammer and nails (or a drill) to make holes

glue

cutting mat

duct tape

metal fasteners, pushpins, clothespins, and pipe cleaners

stapler

scissors

craft knife

yarn

paint and paintbrushes

ruler

permanent markers

pencils and pens

lots of cardboard

PROJECT #1
TAMBOURINE

Nothings keeps the beat like the happy jingle of a tambourine. Start your very own band with this cardboard instrument keeping time!

SUPPLIES

- craft knife
- oatmeal container
- cutting mat
- lined paper

- hole punch
- duct tape
- permanent markers

- paint and paintbrush
- pipe cleaners
- bells

1 Using a craft knife, cut out a ring of cardboard around the lid of an oatmeal container. (Save the rest of the container for the crafts on pages 10-11!)

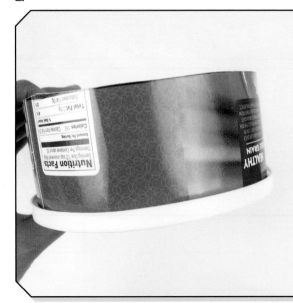

An easy way to make sure your ring is even is to cut out a rectangle from lined paper. Line it up against the edge of your container and trace around the paper for a line to follow while cutting.

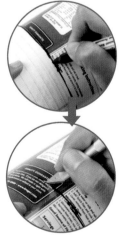

Use a hole punch to punch pairs of holes around the cardboard cylinder.

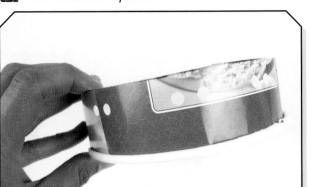

 Use duct tape and permanent markers to decorate the lid (face) of the tambourine.

 Paint the cardboard cylinder. Once the paint dries, attach the lid.

 Use pipe cleaners to attach bells to the outside of the tambourine.

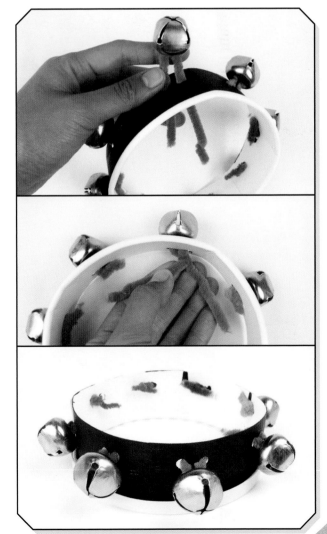

PROJECT #2
DRUM SET

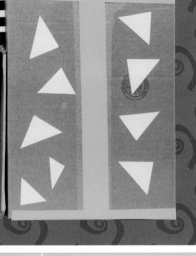

Every good band needs a drummer. Without one, who would keep the beat? Create your own drum set with tin cans and boxes, and pound your way to an awesome rock concert!

SUPPLIES

- cardboard boxes in various sizes
- duct tape
- scissors

- used tin cans in various sizes
- cork from a bottle

- disposable aluminum pie plates
- pushpins

- drill (or hammer and nail)
- yarn
- chopsticks

1 Tape a cardboard box shut. Decorate it with shapes cut from the different-sized boxes.

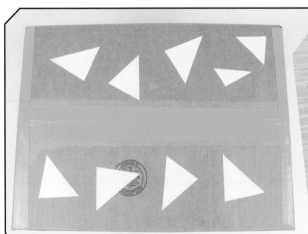

TIP
You can also use stickers, crayons, or markers to decorate your boxes.

2 To make a tin can "cowbell," wash and dry the can. Decorate it with duct tape.

3 (To make a cymbal and stand)

Attach a cork to the top of a cardboard box. Attach a pie plate to the top with a pushpin. Use duct tape to tape the box shut. Then decorate it.

Attach the cork with a pin from inside the box.

TIP

Don't have a pie plate? You can use a disposable baking pan.

4 (To make tin can "bells")

Wash your tin cans well. Drill two holes in the bottom of each can. For each can you plan on using, drill two corresponding holes in your cardboard box. Use pieces of yarn to tie the cans to the inside of your box. Decorate your box and cans with duct tape.

5 Arrange your various instruments, and play them with chopsticks!

TIP

Don't own chopsticks? Use pencils, markers, or any long sturdy sticks instead!

Don't forget to decorate and seal other boxes to join your set!

9

PROJECT #3

BANJO AND UKULELE

Ready to transform the leftover oatmeal container into not just one, but two stringed instruments? Time to make a banjo and ukulele and get your band playing!

SUPPLIES

- scissors
- leftover oatmeal container (from pages 6-7)
- pencil
- 2 cereal boxes
- corrugated cardboard
- tacky glue
- craft knife
- cutting mat
- paint and paintbrush
- permanent marker
- drill (or hammer and nail)
- 8 rubber bands
- duct tape

STEPS FOR UKULELE

TIP
Save the bottom of the oatmeal container to make the banjo!

1. (To make the body) Cut out two cardboard rings of similar width from the oatmeal container.

To make a ring that is uniformly wide, refer to step 1 on page 6.

2. Place one ring on top of the other so they overlap a little bit. Mark the two places where the rings overlap. Cut two slits where you marked the cardboard. Slide the two rings together to create a ukulele frame.

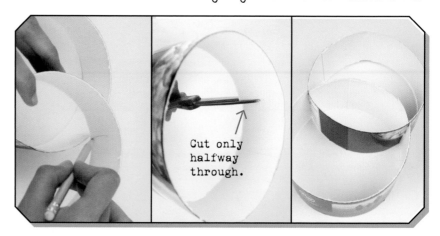

Cut only halfway through.

Trace your frame onto a piece of cereal box cardboard two times. Cut out. One piece will be the back of your instrument. One will be the front. Cut out a small hole from the front of your ukulele.

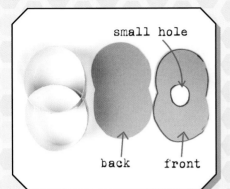

small hole

back   front

 Cut out two small rectangles from cardboard. They should be about 2 inches (5 cm) long.

These will be your bridge pieces.

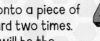 Cut out two long rectangles from cardboard. They should be about 9 inches (23 cm) long. Glue the two pieces together.

This is the fingerboard.

 Use a craft knife to cut a hole in the top of the frame.

 Glue the back of the ukulele to the frame.

 Now you can decorate your ukulele parts with paint and marker.

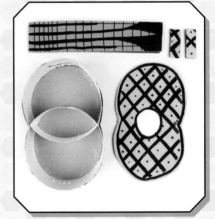

 Glue on the two bridge pieces.

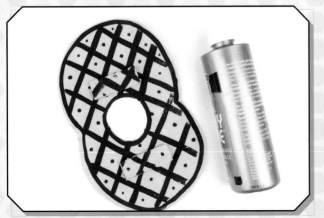

 Ask an adult to drill four holes on top and below the bridge pieces.

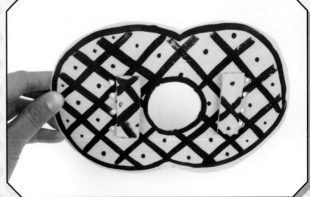

11

11 Cut four rubber bands in half. Tie them together and push the other ends through two top holes. Then stretch the bands over the sound hole and push them through the two bottom corresponding holes. Tie the rubber bands together to hold them in place. Do the same process for the remaining pairs of holes.

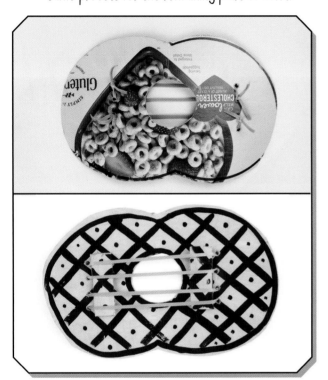

12 Push the cardboard rectangle through the hole. Carefully tear apart the two pieces of cardboard for about ½ inch (1.3 cm). Tape it to the inside of the instrument.

Don't forget to attach the front of the ukulele with tacky glue. Now you're ready to play!

STEPS FOR BANJO

1 Cut out a circle in the oatmeal container's bottom piece. This will be the opening in the banjo.

2 Trace the banjo body onto a piece of cereal box. Cut out the resulting circle. This will be the back of your banjo.

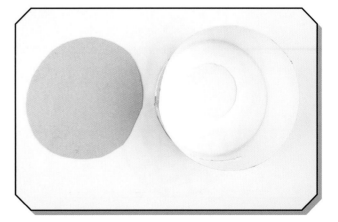

3 (Make the bridge and fingerboard pieces)

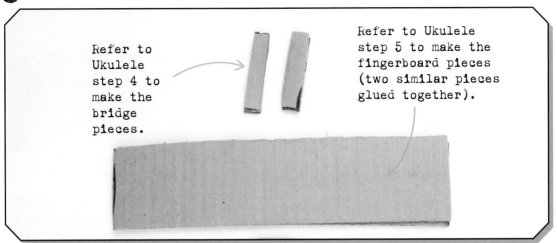

Refer to Ukulele step 4 to make the bridge pieces.

Refer to Ukulele step 5 to make the fingerboard pieces (two similar pieces glued together).

 4 Use a marker or paint to decorate all of the banjo parts.

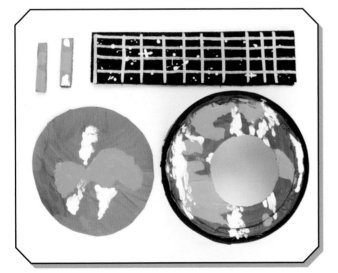

5 Glue one bridge piece on top of the cutout circle. Glue the other bridge piece just below the cutout circle. Ask an adult to drill four holes on top and four holes on the bottom of the banjo head.

6 String your banjo as shown in Ukulele step 11.

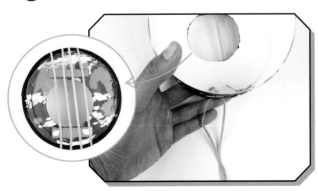

7 Attach the fingerboard as shown in Ukulele step 12. Now get playing!

PROJECT #1

RING / CAP TOSS GAME

Step right up, it's time to play some games! Now you can make your own version of a ring toss or cap game with an egg carton and some duct tape. Who knew fun would be so easy?

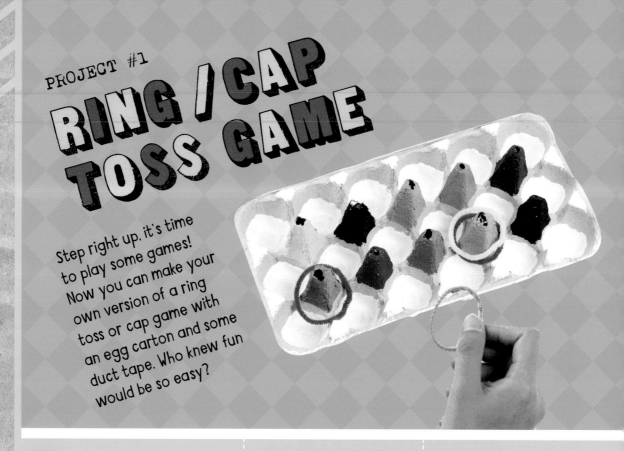

- 2 cardboard egg cartons
- paint and paintbrush
- scissors
- duct tape (or packing tape)
- hot glue (optional)
- pipe cleaners
- caps from squeeze pouches or milk jugs (or ping-pong balls)

 Cut the lids off your egg cartons.

 Paint your egg cartons.

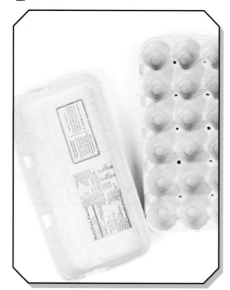

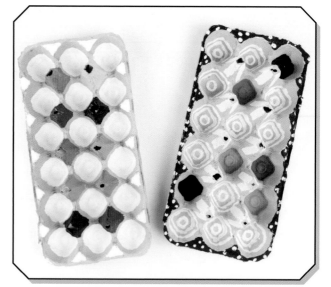

To make the Cap Toss Game stand up, cut out three rectangular pieces from the egg carton lid. Tape them together to form a triangle.

 Hot glue your triangle to the back of your painted egg carton.

 To make the rings for the ring toss game, twist the two ends of the pipe cleaner together to form circles.

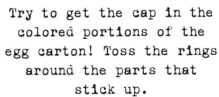

Try to get the cap in the colored portions of the egg carton! Toss the rings around the parts that stick up.

NOW START TOSSING!

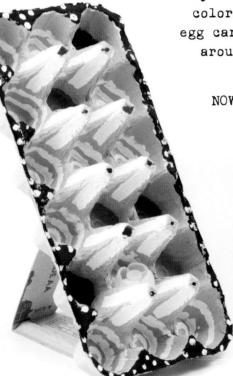

PROJECT #3

SHOOTING DISK GAME

How good are you at shooting milk jug caps? This fun carnival game pits you against a partner. See how many caps you can shoot into this funny man's belly while an animated mustache blocks your moves!

SUPPLIES

- scissors
- craft knife
- cutting mat
- corrugated cardboard box
- corrugated cardboard
- ruler
- milk caps
- pencil
- drill (or hammer and nail)
- metal fastener
- paint and paintbrush
- permanent markers

Cut out a slot in both the front and back of your box. The slot should be big enough for a milk cap disk to easily slide through.

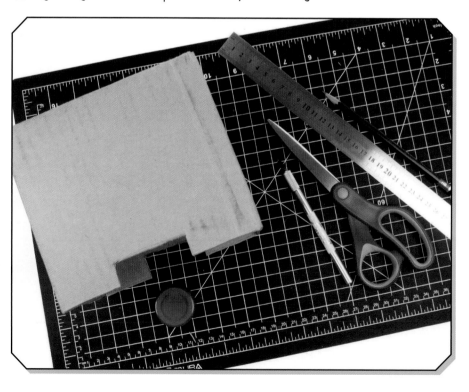

2 Cut out a mustache from corrugated cardboard.

3 Drill a hole in your box and mustache. The hole should be big enough to hold a fastener.

It should also be placed so that the mustache will effectively block caps.

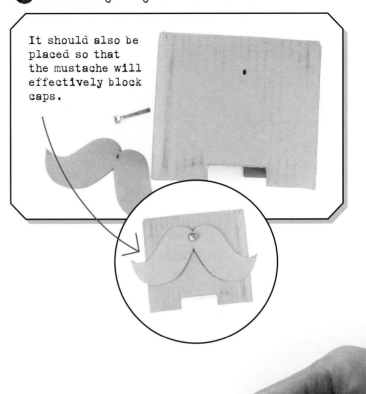

4 Use markers and paint to decorate your man.

Now have your partner swing the mustache while you try shooting the milk caps — then switch off. Who can get the most in?

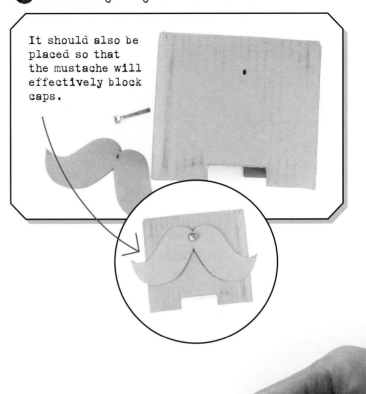

17

PROJECT #1

ACADEMY AWARDS

Did you write, act, or shoot a blockbuster movie? That's great! Let's celebrate your hard work and creativity with your very own award made of cardboard and duct tape!

SUPPLIES

- pencil and paper
- corrugated cardboard
- scissors
- tacky glue
- craft knife
- cutting mat
- small corrugated cardboard box
- black duct tape
- gold paint
- paintbrush
- permanent marker

1. Draw a template for your award. It should include a statue on top and a tab on the bottom. This will ensure that your statue slides into the award's base. Use your template to cut out three identical statues.

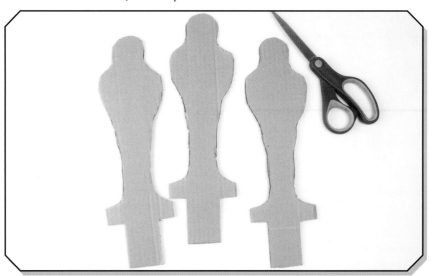

2 Use tacky glue to glue your cardboard pieces on top of each other.

TIP
To make sure they dry flat, place the cardboard underneath some heavy books.

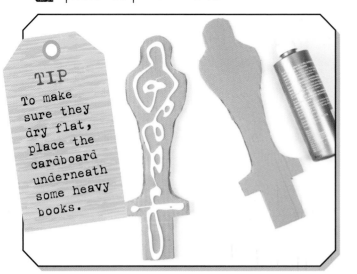

3 Now we're going to make the base. Cut the bottom off a small box. Then cut out a slit in the middle of your box's top. Also cut out a piece of cardboard that is slightly larger than your base.

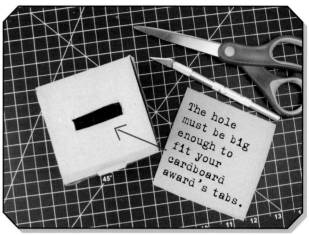

The hole must be big enough to fit your cardboard award's tabs.

4 Cover the two base pieces with black duct tape. You can also paint the base black.

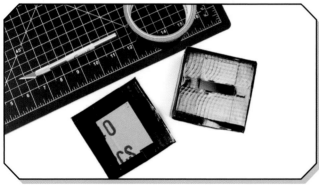

5 Paint your statue. Once the paint dries, use permanent markers to add details. This will make your award really pop.

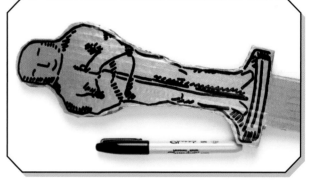

6 Slide your statue's tab into your base's cutout hole. The statue will be a bit wobbly, so cut out a cardboard cross piece to stabilize it.

The statue's tab should fit into the slit.

TIP
To further secure the statue in place, tape the two cross pieces together.

7 Tape your base onto the slightly larger piece of cardboard.

PROJECT #2

MOVIE CLAPPER

Ready to begin your career in filmmaking? You'll need to mark the beginning and ends of movie scenes. Make yourself a clapper board and start shooting!

SUPPLIES

- scissors
- pencil
- corrugated cardboard
- drill
- tacky glue
- black and white paint
- paintbrush
- metal fastener
- decoupage glue (optional)
- white pencil (optional)
- sponge brush (optional)

1 Cut out the shapes for your clapper: two identical body parts, two identical large rectangles, and two identical small rectangles.

small rectangles 1 & 2

large rectangle 1

large rectangle 2

body part 1

body part 2

Drill holes through the corners of the large rectangles. Then drill holes through the circular bit of the body parts.

 Glue the two body parts to each other, the large rectangles to each other, and the small rectangles to each other. Glue the small rectangles on top of the body. Make sure the holes line up when gluing.

Make sure the holes line up with both pieces of each shape.

 Once the glue dries, paint everything black. Use white paint to add details like the stripes, lines, or words.

TIP
To make the sign shiny and sturdy, cover it with a layer of decoupage glue.

 Assemble the clapperboard. Use a fastener to attach the large rectangle on top of the body. Now you're ready to shoot a movie!

PROJECT #3

MINI TV

Ever think about shooting your own television show or movie? Here's a way to see your dream come true! Make your own cardboard TV and watch your stories come to life!

SUPPLIES

- shoe box
- craft knife
- cutting mat
- ruler
- drill
- metal fasteners
- paper
- markers
- duct tape
- pencil/ chopsticks (taller than the height of your TV/ shoebox)
- scissors
- caps from squeeze pouches, milk jugs, or other
- duct tape
- tape
- Styrofoam block

Cut out a rectangle from your box. This will be your television's screen.

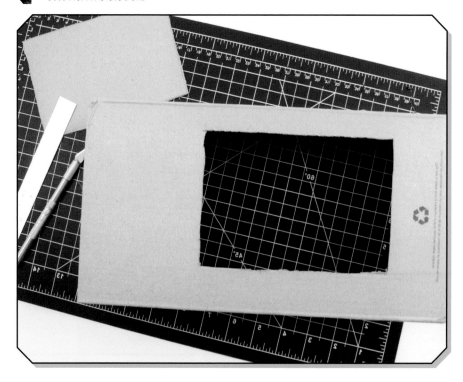

Drill two holes on the top of your television. They should be slightly farther apart than the width of your screen. They should also fit your two pencils.

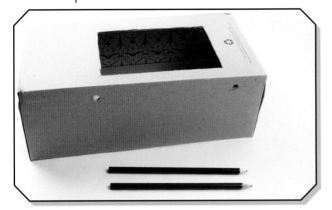

 Drill two holes in the front of your TV. Drill matching holes in two caps. The holes should be big enough to fit your fasteners.

TIP

Skip the drilling and just draw on knobs and buttons.

 Cut out a long sheet of paper to be your storyboard. It's height should be slightly larger than your screen's height. Draw on your story.

TIP

Don't have a long sheet of paper? Tape together several pieces of shorter paper.

 Decorate your television with markers and duct tape. Fasten on your buttons (from step 3).

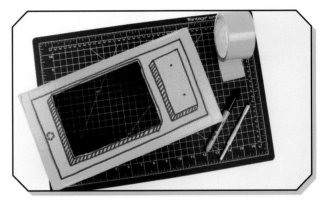

 Place your pencils through the two holes. Tape one end of your story to one pencil. Curl the roll of paper around that pencil. Then tape the other end to the other pencil. Now cut out a piece of Styrofoam. Stick your pencils into the Styrofoam to hold them in place. Tape your Styrofoam down. Now twist the pencil to play your show!

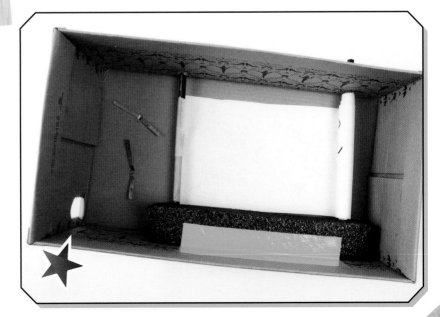

DUCT TAPE BOW TIE

To put on a magic show, you've got to look the part. Whip up these cool and colorful duct tape bow ties to get you on your way!

SUPPLIES

- scissors or craft knife
- cutting mat
- ruler
- duct tape (black, green, gold, yellow, silver)
- hook and loop fastener (optional)

1. Cut a 16-inch (41-cm) strip of duct tape and place it sticky-side up. Fold one third over, then the other third. Use a craft knife or scissors to trim the ends. This will be the strap.

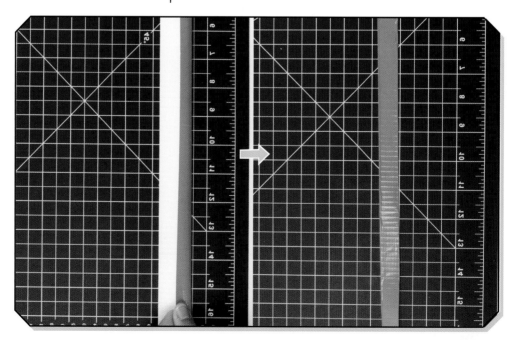

Cut two 5-inch (13-cm) pieces of duct tape. This will be for the bow.

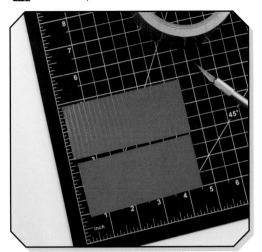

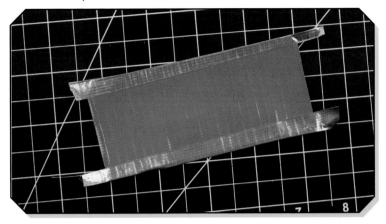 Place one on top of the other so that the sticky sides are together. To add a different color trim, wrap both long sides of your duct tape piece with thin strips of different-colored duct tape. Trim off any excess bits.

 Pinch the middle to make a bow shape.

First fold your duct tape strip in half. Then fold both sides inward.

 Use a thin piece of tape to help the bow keep its shape. Then, use a bigger piece of tape to tie the bow onto your strap.

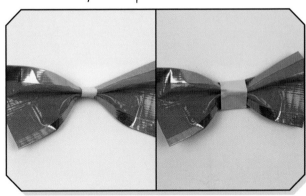

Use a thin piece of tape to tape both sides together around your neck.

Experiment making more bows with different-colored duct tape!

TIP

Instead of tape, use a hook and loop fastener — then you can wear your bow tie over and over again!

PROJECT #2

MAGIC HAT

Every magician needs a swanky top hat. Where else will you store your rabbits? Make a great hat from cardboard for this awesome craft!

 1 Cut open your cereal box. Cut out a cardboard rectangle big enough to wrap around your head.

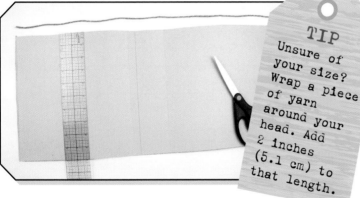

 2 Tightly curl your cardboard into a large tube. This will make your hat cylindrical.

TIP
Unsure of your size? Wrap a piece of yarn around your head. Add 2 inches (5.1 cm) to that length.

 3 Make sure your piece of cardboard wraps around your head. If it does, staple it together.

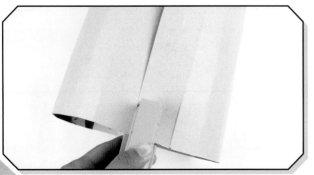

 4 Trace your cylinder onto a cereal box.

Trace a larger circle around your traced circle.

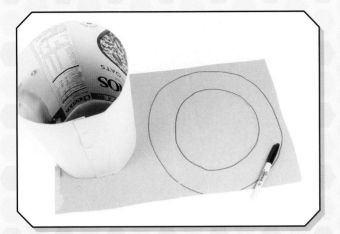

 Cut out the larger circle and the smaller circle. The smaller circle will be the top of the hat and the larger circle will be the brim.

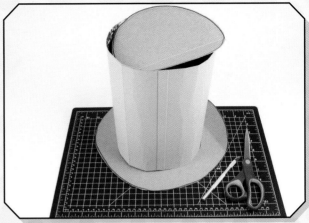

 To attach the hat to the brim, cut out tabs in the bottom of your cylinder. Slide the cylinder into your brim. Duct tape the tabs to the brim.

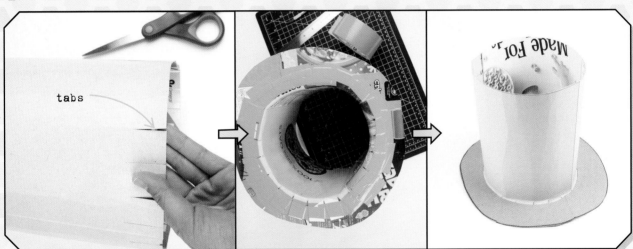

tabs

8 Attach the top of the hat with tacky glue.

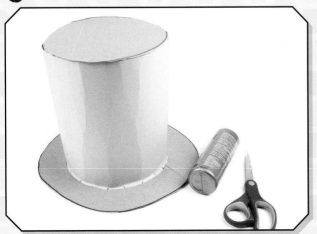

9 Paint the hat and add a strip of duct tape.

PROJECT #3

MAGIC BOX

Ever dream of having real magic powers? Wouldn't it be cool to make things disappear? Well, with this super rad magic box, you can! Start your magic training here!

SUPPLIES

- large tin can
- smaller tin can
- cardboard box
- duct tape
- craft knife

- cutting mat
- scissors
- black paint
- paintbrush
- brown paper

- bag (or a thick sheet of paper)
- ruler
- permanent markers

- pencil
- small object (should fit inside the smaller tin can)

 Make sure that the small tin can fits inside the large tin can, and the large tin can fits inside of your box.

 Wash and dry your tin cans. Ask an adult to cut off the bottom of the larger tin can.

 Use duct tape to decorate your larger can.

 Paint the inside of your box black. Cut out a large rectangular piece of brown paper to wrap around the smaller can. Paint it black.

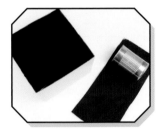

 Trim the painted paper so that it fits around your smaller can.

 Tape the painted paper onto your can with clear tape. Cut out a smaller black rectangle from your remaining painted paper. Tape the smaller sheet inside of your can.

TIP

To fit the can exactly, roll it along the paper and use a pencil to trace the edges of the can while you roll.

7 Create a design for the front of the box with a couple small-sized, cut-out portions. This will allow the audience to glimpse inside. Use a craft knife and cut out portions from the box's front. Decorate the box with permanent markers and duct tape. Make sure to keep the cut-out portions exposed.

These shaded parts outside the star will be the cutouts.

LET'S MAKE THINGS APPEAR FROM THIN AIR!

BEFORE YOU GATHER YOUR AUDIENCE: Place your colorful can inside of your box. Place your black can inside of your colorful can. Then put a tiny object (toy, scarf, egg, crayon, or whatever) inside of your black can.

BEFORE YOU PERFORM THE TRICK: Place the box on an elevated surface. Seat the audience lower than your box (important!). Tell them that you own a magic box.

1 Carefully pull out the large can and reveal that it is just a hollow tube.

2 Carefully place the large can back inside your box. Make sure that it doesn't touch your black can.

3 Say some magic words and then reach into your box.

4 Carefully pull out your hidden object!

MAKERSPACE TIPS

Download tips and tricks for using this book and others in a library makerspace. Visit www.capstonepub.com/dabblelabresources

READ MORE

Harbo, Christopher. *Origami Explosion: Scorpions, Whales, Boxes, and More.* Origami Paperpalooza. North Mankato, Minn.: Capstone Press, 2015.

Sjonger, Rebecca. *Maker Projects for Kids Who Love Paper Engineering.* Be a Maker. New York: Crabtree Publishing Company, 2016.

Ventura, Marne. *Awesome Paper Projects You Can Create.* Imagine It, Build It. North Mankato, Minn.: Capstone Press, 2016.

INTERNET SITES

FactHound offers a safe, fun way to find Internet sites related to this book. All of the sites on FactHound have been researched by our staff.

Here's all you do:
Visit www.facthound.com
Just type in 9781515793120 and go!

 Check out projects, games and lots more at
www.capstonekids.com

ABOUT THE AUTHOR

LESLIE MANLAPIG

Leslie is a full-time mom and sometimes puppeteer who adores books, donuts, and the color yellow. She's always on the lookout for new ways to play and make things with kids. You can read about her family's creative and crafty adventures on her blog www.PinkStripeySocks.com.

Dabble Lab Books are published by Capstone Press.
1710 Roe Crest Drive
North Mankato, Minnesota 56003
www.mycapstone.com

Cataloging-in-Publication Data is available
on the Library of Congress website.
ISBN 978-1-5157-9312-0 (library binding)
ISBN 978-1-5157-9315-1 (eBook PDF)

Editors: Anna Butzer and Shelly Lyons
Designer: Aruna Rangarajan
Media Researcher: Tracy Cummins
Production Specialist: Tori Abraham

Image credits: All photos by Leslie Manlapig and
Enrico Manlapig, except the following: Shutterstock:
abeadev, Design Element, Africa Studio, 3 (hand, phone),
Jakub Krechowicz, Design Element, KannaA, Design
Element, Kiselev Andrey Valerevich, Design Element,
KsanaGraphica, Design Element, Picsfive, Design Element,
Winai Tepsuttinun, Back Cover (box), Design Element

Printed and bound in the United States of America.
010750S18